TAC

A Pictorial History of
the USAF Tactical Air
Forces 1970-1977

by Lou Drendel

squadron/signal publications

Photo Credits

Lou Drendel
Norman E. Taylor
Scott Brown
Jerry Geer
Ken Buchanan
Charles Mayer
Shinichi Ohtaki
Jim Sullivan
USAF
Dave Menard
McDonnell Douglas
Grumman
Boeing

Foreword

The sub-title on the cover reads; "A Pictorial History of the USAF Tactical Air Forces 1970-1977." It could just as well read: "A Pictorial Survey of the aircraft of USAF Tactical Air Forces 1970-1977." or, "TAC's transition from yesterday to tommorrow." Both would be true. In fact, it was for the latter reason that I chose to portray TAC in the 70's. At the beginning of this decade, only three new aircraft types had been added to TAC's inventory in the previous ten years. (A-7D, F-111, and OV-10) Of the dozens of types that were operated by TAC, many dated back as far as World War II.

The Air War in Vietnam had thrust tactical air into the future, with new tactics and technology, and it was obvious that new aircraft were needed to accomodate the resultant changes. Some of the "new" aircraft are merely modifications of existing types. Others are all new, and have performance margins built into them that will more than likely assure their continued role in TAC to the end of this century. They are all here, and they provide a panoramic view of TAC's diversity and flexibility, past, present, and future.

Introduction

The Tactical Air Command was formed on 21 March 1946. It was one of three major combat commands of the newly designated United States Air Force. It was awarded "major" status in recognition of the job tactical air power had done in World War II, but very few planners in 1946 believed that tactical air power would ever play a major role in warfare again. The emphasis was on atomic weaponry, and the maintenance of a strategic nuclear deterrent force. Consequently, SAC received most of the attention, and funds, in the new Air Force.

When the Russians achieved atomic capability in 1949, more emphasis was shifted to the third major combat command of the Air Force . . . Air Defense Command. Another event of that year added fuel to the fires of advocacy burning in the hearts of proponents of tactical air power. The formation of the North Atlantic Treaty Organization was recognition of mutual responsibilities in the defense of western Europe. The fact that the Russians had nuclear capability, and might one day achieve nuclear parity, making nuclear warfare an Armageddon that no one would survive, led military planners to consider the alternative . . . limited warfare. Planners on the other side of the Iron Curtain had been more than considering the possibility of limited war . . . they had been planning it, and in June 1950 the first "limited war" broke out in Korea.

One of the theoretical problems which had hindered the growth of TAC was the feeling that jet aircraft were too fast to provide accurate close air support. Since close air support was the life blood of TAC, and the jet engine was undoubtedly the only power plant that would be considered by the best designers of the day, TAC stagnated. Korea proved beyond a doubt that pinpoint accuracy could be achieved with jets, as the F-80s and F-84s provided the bulk of close air support for United Nations ground forces.

When the Korean War reached its strategically inconclusive end, TAC had proven two important points which would eventually make it the largest and most diverse of all Air Force commands. Its mission had been justified, and the realization had been reached that the mission could and must be performed with the most modern aircraft and weapons available to USAF. With its mission firmly established as indispensible to United States interests, TAC was now faced with the need for world-wide mobility, and the ability to deploy quickly to operational areas.

In 1954, General O.P. Weyland assumed command of TAC. General Weyland was a visionary who was prepared to adopt and adapt the latest techniques to keep TAC at the forefront of United States military policy. He pushed aerial refueling, and the development of the C-130 turboprop transport.

The century series of fighters was coming into the inventory of the Air Force, and with this, TAC's mission became multi-faceted. The F-100 became the first U.S. fighter to exceed the speed of sound in level flight, and TAC was using it as both strike and air-superiority fighter. The RF-101 provided unparalleled capability for tactical reconnaissance. The F-104's career in TAC was short-lived due to its limited range, but it was the first of the lightweight fighters and was without peer in the air-superiority regime. The F-105 didn't make it as a nuclear bomber, but low-level speed and range made it the backbone of the war against North Vietnam in the 60s, and led to the development of strike fighters tailored to the low-level high speed interdiction mission. The introduction of these new fighters, coupled with a series of peacetime joint Air Force-Army maneuvers in the mid 50s, served to expand TAC's role and to prepare it for a limited war which would dwarf all previous wars . . . in U.S. history . . . both in time and expenditure.

To prove the efficacy of aerial refueling, and to demonstrate its global mobility, TAC in 1954 began rotating fighter squadrons to Europe on a six month basis. By 1959 this program had achieved an annual rotational rate of 1,200 aircraft, requiring more than 3,500 refuellings. In the space of five years what had seemed a risky operation had become a routinely employed operational technique.

Perhaps the most important development of the mid-50s, inrespect to TAC's newly mandated global mobility, was the activation of the Nineteenth Air Force. Unlike Ninth and Twelfth Air Forces, which are conventional subordinate command organizations, the Nineteenth was given a specific and challenging mission, specifically; to "Be prepared to deploy any and all assigned units to any theater or area in the world as might be directed and be capable of exercising operational control of attached units upon their arrival in the combat zone."

It is difficult to imagine a more complex or difficult mission to perform at a moment's notice. The key to success lay in what was then known as the "Composite Air Strike Force", and it was no coincidence that the Nineteenth's first commander was one of the architects of CASF. Major General Henry Viccellio recognized the difficulties involved . . . CASF depended upon prepackaged "fly-away-kits", which would contain everything needed to operate in a given area for a specified time, but the kits had to be continually modified to keep pace with changing world hot-spots. (What good would Berlin kits do if the trouble erupted in Korea?) But he also recognized and stated the absolute necessity for the CASF concept in these words; "The very location of potential hot spots highlights a special CASF characteristic. It is by nature complementary to other American forces—when the Soviets increase their pressure on remote hot spots, we must intensify our counter measures with SAC, with far-ranging naval carrier forces in Europe and the Far East—this is our big stick concept in keeping things limited—versatility is to us far more than a glittering generality—it enables us to produce the exact degree of force at the right place at the right time."

The Nineteenth had two years to perfect CASF before it was called upon to prove its viability in an actual crisis, and then it was not one crisis, but two . . . in rapid succession. The Lebanon crisis of July 1958 saw TAC deploy jet fighters to Turkey within twelve hours of receiving the order to move. Shortly afterwards, the crisis of the Formosa Strait gave TAC the opportunity to show that it could move men and machines even greater distances in time to squelch a potentially dangerous situation. And in the midst of these two crisis deployments, TAC continued to fulfill routine responsibilities by rotating a squadron of F-100s to Europe.

1958 was a year of further expansion of TAC's role, as it accepted the task of advanced flight training from ATC. Pilots with less than five hundred hours went to Luke or Williams AFB for honing of their skills, while the foundation was laid for the even more advanced Fighter Weapons School at Nellis AFB. It was also the year in which more sophisticated cooperation between air and ground forces became a goal which would be realized three years later with the formation of the U.S. Strike Command.

General Walter C. Sweeney, Jr. assumed command of TAC in 1961, and immediately set about the task of establishing a more positive command and control system. The result was TAC's Command Post at Langley AFB. He also reorganized TAC's Ninth and Twelfth Air Forces along geographical lines, the Ninth assuming command of all bases east of the Mississippi, the Twelfth all bases to the west.

Cold War crises continued to provide TAC with opportunities to develop and prove its skills. The Berlin Crisis of October 1961 resulted in the recall of more than 26,000 Air Force Reserve and Air National Guard personnel, which included six tactical fighter wings, one reconnaissance wing, and two troop carrier wings. Within a month of recall, the Air National Guard deployed 210 fighters and recce planes to Europe, proving that the "citizen soldiers" of TAC were an effective force.

A year later the most serious threat to United States security since the end of World War II occured, with the introduction of Soviet missiles into Cuba. TAC's contribution to the quarantine of Cuba, which eventually led to "the other guy blinking first", was over 1,000 aircraft. Combat missions were flown by RF-101 reconnaissance jets, covered by TAC fighters. Other TAC fighters remained on alert and flew practice missions to prepare for the eventuality of war, while a fleet of TAC C-130s provided tactical airlift of men and material.

Two years later the 464th Troop Carrier Wing, based at Pope AFB, N.C., airdropped and airlanded a battalion of Belgian paratroops in rebel-held territory in the Congo to effect the rescue of 1,500 hostages. The 464th flew more than 1,000 sorties in evacuating refugees from Stanleyville and Paulis to Leopoldville. For its mission of mercy, the 464th won the MacKay Trophy for 1964. But the humanitarian mission of the 464th was overshadowed by events on the other side of the World. TAC was becoming involved in a shooting war in Vietnam.

TAC had shown through several Cold War crisis that it could react with the appropriate amount of force quickly. But it was dawning on U.S. political leaders that one of these times merely waving the big stick might not suffice. The United States might be called upon to actually fight another limited war. The new emphasis within the Communist camp was on "wars of liberation", wherein guerilla forces were covertly supplied with the means to overthrow established governments friendly to the United States. To counter this, military planners were given the task of forming counter-insurgency forces. In 1962 TAC established the USAF Special Air Warfare Center at Eglin AFB, Florida to develop new techniques and tactics for airborne counter-insurgency operations.

Vietnam provided the proving grounds for much of the counter-insurgency theory of the early sixties. When the Gulf of Tonkin incident exploded the war into a more conventional struggle, TAC began what was to be a long and challenging task. Though not directly involved in promulgation of the war, TAC supplied men and aircraft to PACAF, and developed tactics and weapons to meet changing needs in the war zone. Unfortunately, the war, costly as it was, was being fought with funds that should have gone into force modernization. As the decade of the 70s dawned, and "Vietnamization" of the war effort was permitting withdrawal of United States resources, TAC began to recover many of its aircraft from Southeast Asia. The airplanes returning were 1950s vintage F-100s and F-105s, which had served for five years in the toughest air defense environment in history. They were tired airplanes, badly in need of replacement.

The stage was set for one of the most exciting periods in the history of TAC and USAF tactical air power. For, if USAF had suffered a lack of new equipment because of Vietnam, it had reaped a cornucopia of actual tactical experience, which would allow application of new technologies in the final convulsion of the Vietnam Air War, and make development of the new and long-overdue weapons systems possible on a scale not seen since the heyday of Cold War fever.

Aggressor T-38 being made ready for a mission. (USAF)

TAC in the 70s

The Tactical Air Command is the United States Air Force's mobile strike force, able to deploy US general purpose air forces anywhere in the world on a moment's notice for tactical air operations in support of national security requirements. The key to TAC's mobility is the "Bare Base" concept. The bare base is defined as one having a runway, taxiway, parking ramps, and a source of fresh water. Bare base traces its roots to the CASF concept of the 50s, but whereas CASF required an active airfield for its implementation, Bare Base is just what its name implies. It adds over 1,400 potential operational airfields, worldwide, to TAC's list of areas of deployment.

The big U.S. buildup in Vietnam, which required construction of several air bases to support tactical airpower, triggered a study aimed at avoidance of costly permanent base construction in future deployments. The 1965 study resulted in the reorganization of TAC into self-sustaining squadron-sized units. New equipment was designed to provide facilities never before available to mobile units, all of it packaged in air-transportable modules. Included are facilities such as hangars, barracks, dining halls, communications centers, dispensaries, and maintenance shops. This equipment is designed to have a five year life span, figuring two deployments per year. (Life span of the equipment is doubled when stored, and not used.)

Throughout the present decade, TAC headquarters at Langley AFB, Virginia, has directed the activities of two numbered air forces within the United States. The 9th Air Force, Shaw AFB, South Carolina, and the 12th Air Force, Bergstrom AFB, Texas, direct TAC operations in the United States. TAC's U.S. Air Force Southern Air Division (USAFSO), headquartered at Albrook AFB, Canal Zone, exercises command jurisdiction over USAF resources throughout Latin America. TAC also directs the activities of two specialized centers. Each is assigned to serve as TAC's expert in its respective field. The Tactical Air Warfare Center, Eglin AFB, Florida develops and tests new concepts, doctrine, tactics, penetration aids, and weapons designed for tactical air forces. TAWC was formed in 1963 for the express purpose of improving upon the Air Force's capability to support Army forces in joint field maneuvers. With the advent of the Vietnam War, its efforts were directed at more specifically defined goals, including operational testing and evaluation of specific armaments, night operations, combat support operations, reconnaissance, electronic warfare, tactical airlift, and command and control.

The Tactical Fighter Weapons Center, Nellis AFB, Nevada, is the graduate school for concepts, doctrine, tactics, and testing of new equipment and munitions designed for tactical fighter operations. During a 1976 visit to Nellis, I talked with its commander, Major General James A. Knight, Jr. He prefaced his remarks concerning the center with this comment; "I feel especially privileged to have this assignment at this time, for I think that this is the most significant and exciting period in the history of TAC." TFWC is the parent unit of the 57th Fighter Weapons Wing, which runs the Fighter Weapons School. FWS is the graduate school for fighter pilots. It is considered a large step forward in one's career to be picked to attend. Graduates of the school return to their units as the resident expert in the latest tactics, and are expected to pass on their knowledge to the unit. TFWC is also the parent unit of the 57th Combat Support Group, 4486th Test Squadron at Edwards AFB, and Operating Location AA, at Luke AFB, Arizona. Nellis AFB is also the home of the most widely recognized Air Force unit, the Thunderbirds aerial demonstration team.

The most widely dispersed TAC unit is the 2nd Aircraft Delivery Group, with detachments located throughout the world. This organization is responsible for command and control of worldwide flight delivery of aircraft for the USAF, and to friendly foreign governments. TAC displayed the quick reaction capabilities of this unit during the 1973 Mideast war. Within sixteen hours of the decision to provide additional aircraft to the Israelis, F-4s and C-130s were airborne enroute to Israel.

Also under control of TAC headquarters are the 552nd Airborne Warning and Control Wing, Tinker AFB, Oklahoma, which operates one of the newest and most sophisticated aircraft in the USAF Inventory, the E-3A AWACS, the 7th Airborne Command and Control Squadron, flying C-130s out of Keesler AFB, Mississippi, and the 8th Tactical Deployment Control Squadron, flying EC-135s from Seymour Johnson AFB, N.C.

TAC is the lead command of all USAF Tactical Air Forces, which include U.S. Air Forces Europe (USAFE), and Pacific Air Forces (PACAF). it is also the gaining command for 50,000 Air Reserve and Air National Guard personnel in 99 units across the nation.

TAC is USAF's most versatile command, and in this decade has operated a multitude of aircraft types and sub-types in support of a wide variety of combat and peacetime missions. The missions of TAC provide the chapter titles for this pictorial history of the USAF Tactical Air Forces in the 1970s.

F-4C of the 57th FWW at Nellis bears the name of Commander of USAF Tactical Fighter Weapons Center, M/G James A. Knight, Jr. F-5 silhouettes on splitter vane indicate that he has "shot down" enough aggressors to be an ace. (USAF)

THE FLAGS OF TAC

One of the lessons of the Vietnam War was that run-of-the-mill peacetime training was an inadequate preparation for combat operations. In order to make itself more combat-ready, TAC began to formulate a more realistic training environment in the early 70s. The training programs that have been developed are known as "flags", and they test the performance of all TAC personnel under the stress of a simulated combat environment.

RED FLAG

The Vietnam War confirmed a statistic that had prevailed in all previous wars. If a combat pilot could survive his first ten missions, he developed the combat sense that would dramatically increase his chances of completing his tour. Red Flag is designed as an attempt to give TAC's aircrews those first ten all-important, missions before they are called upon to fight a shooting war.

Red Flag is conducted at Nellis Air Force Base in Nevada to take advantage of the base's isolated desert range areas. The program is operated by personnel from the Air Force's Tactical Fighter Weapons Center.

In the past, air combat training was limited to engagements between aircraft of the same type, using the same tactics. The jock with more training, who knew his airplane a little better, or was able to withstand more Gs usually was the winner. Air to ground weapons training was conducted on the range in a strictly controlled environment, free of any threat to the bombers.

Red Flag has changed that. In a Red Flag exercise, the whole squadron is moved to Nellis, just as it would be to a combat zone. Upon arrival at Nellis, the squadron is immediately given targets to strike on the Nellis ranges. The Nellis range system is capable of simulating all known enemy threats, from AAA to Migs. The squadron is tasked with penetrating the defense, putting its ordnance on target, and returning safely to base. Scoring is done through an elaborate system of radars, computers and communications equipment which is monitored by referees. The strike pilots see threats indicated on their RHAW equipment, and experience the adrenalin-pumping sensation of being jumped by Migs. The Mig threat is simulated by two squadrons of aggressors, who fly the T-38 and F-5. Both of these aircraft approximate the Mig-21 in size and performance, and they are painted in a variety of camouflage patterns. The aggressors use only Soviet tactics in their attacks.

If a pilot is shot down in Red Flag, he doesn't just return to the home drome to sit out the program. He is helicoptered back to the exercise area and left to demonstrate his escape and evasion prowess.

If he isn't shot down, the pilot will go through an intensive de-brief with the "enemy" when he returns, and will get a first hand assessment of his performance. Red Flag has become the most realistic training exercise ever devised. The measure of its success is attested to by the fact that units from the Army, Navy, Marines, and other major Air Forces commands such as SAC are getting in on it. Its effectiveness has encouraged NATO allies to send units of their air forces to participate. If we are called upon to fight another war, coordination between our services and allies will be enhanced because of Red Flag.

BLUE FLAG

Blue Flag is conducted at Eglin AFB, Florida. It provides decision-making training for battle staffs, who are required to assess a simulated enemy air defense system and offensive capability and then apply tactics to neutralize them. The battle staffs utilize intelligence gathering functions; command, control and communications capabilities; and reconnaissance, fighter and strike forces during the manufactured crisis situation.

BLACK FLAG

Black Flag will test the logistics and maintenance functions of a squadron. Two of the methods now under study to implement Black Flag are POMO (Production Oriented Maintenance Organization), which places aircraft maintenance people into smaller self-contained units closely associated with the flying squadrons they would be required to support in combat. POST (Production Oriented Scheduling Techniques) will determine the best ways to schedule maintenance and logistics activities in support of flying requirements.

GREEN FLAG

Green Flag is a combined operations and intelligence program, in which aircrews are assigned specific potential European and Pacific target areas. After receiving its target area, each unit researches the problem, prepares employment scenarios, develops target materials for aircrews, and evaluates intelligence materials on a continuing basis. The completed target scenario is shared with other TAC units having the same basic problem.

GOLD FLAG

Gold Flag stresses accelerated training for less experienced TAC pilots. It is designed to compensate for a projected pilot shortage during the late seventies. It will also help alleviate shortages caused by conversion to new aircraft such as the F-15, A-10, E-3A, and F-16. To accomodate this increased need for pilots, TAC is stepping up the flight training for its less experienced pilots, which in turn will make room for the absorption of a larger number of pilots. To accomplish this accelerated training, TAC will reserve two-thirds of its sorties for less experienced pilots, which will increase their flying time by 30%. Twenty five percent of these pilots will be upgraded to flight lead position. The duties of these pilots will be restricted to those that are considered mission-essential. In short, the new tigers will be receiving the most concentrated and effective training ever given in peacetime, and may be better fighter pilots at 300 hours than their mentors were with 1,000.

Aggressor pilot climbs aboard F-5E. Aggressors first received F-5s when it bacame evident that F-5s destined for South Vietnamese Air Force would not be going to them. F-5 has proven to be a better Mig simulator than the T-38 and will eventually equip all Aggressor squadrons. (USAF)

AIR SUPERIORITY

In each of the last three wars, the initial experience of the American fighter pilot has been similar. America, isolationist by nature, peace-loving at heart, and sometimes incredibly naive where the bad guy's intentions are concerned, has never been properly prepared for the wars that come along. In World War II we overcame an initial enemy advantage in tactics, equipment, and saavy, finally emerging with an overall kill ratio of 1.6 to 1 in our favor. Korea was a little different. They had the advantage in equipment, but we had all those hot fighter pilots left over from World War II. We converted this to a 6.2 to 1 advantage in air-to-air combat kills. We should have learned a lesson from Korea. We didn't. The bad guys continued to build better air superiority machines, while we got sidetracked by our technological superiority. We built missile launching platforms that would protect our cities from bombers and our carriers from fighter-bombers. The star of the Korean War, the F-86 Sabre, was the last pure air superiority fighter designed and built for the Air Force until the F-15 Eagle came along. In the meantime, we were relearning old lessons about the value of air superiority the hard way . . . in a shooting war. The North Vietnamese, with an air force of fewer than 200 airplanes, were making it real tough for us to conduct "Rolling Thunder". Their Mig-17s, 19s, and 21s were demonstrably better air-to-air machines than our Thuds and Phantoms. There were times in the air war over Vietnam that they gave as good as they took. In the meantime, we were acquiring valuable experience in the art of air-to-air, and we were finding out that the Phantom could fight in the air superiority role.

In the hiatus between the end of "Rolling Thunder" in 1968, and the onset of "Linebacker" in 1972, some very serious thinking was done in the air-to-air community. It was obvious that a new fighter was needed, and the F-15 was contracted for. In the meantime, we had to find some ways of fighting with what we had. The first attempts were logical enough, and consisted of scheduling of air combat training with other units, flying different aircraft. This was known as DACT (Dissimilar Air Combat Training). The F-106 turned out to be the star of this show, and a lot of people thought it would make a great Mig-21 simulator . . . if it wasn't so big. DACT had made its mark . . . it was more than just a temporary exercise for the die-hard G-pulling fighter jock . . . it was a program that paid dividends in the final months of the Vietnam War, and led to the eventual formation of a permanent unit to train TAC aircrews in fighting air-to-air against enemy tactics.

The Aggressors were activated as a squadron-sized unit in November 1972 as the 64th Fighter Weapons Squadron. (The new Aggressor units will be known as Tactical Fighter Training Aggressor Squadrons.) Their airplane was the Northrop T-38 Talon. Small, lightly wing loaded, with good initial acceleration, the T-38 was the closest thing to a Mig-21 in the USAF inventory. The first Aggressor pilots were hand-picked for their experience and air-to-air aptitude. Because of this, the unit was able to come up with a program, pull together all of the logistical support needed, and make its first deployment with eight months of its formation.

What does it take to become an Aggressor pilot? Preferences vary from unit to unit, but basically, commanders want pilots that have had a couple of tours in a unit with a primary air-to-air mission, and graduates of the Fighter Weapons School are certainly high on the list. Checking out as an Aggressor pilot takes somewhere in the neighborhood of six months, and entails a minimum of 40 air-to-air rides in either the T-38 or the F-5. The curriculum consists of: 1. Learning to max perform the T-38 or F-5. 2. Basic Fighter Maneuvers in the T-38/F-5, wherein the student fights one-on-one with an instructor in another like aircraft. 3. Two vs. One, where a student learns to coordinate the attack with a wingman against one adversary. 4. Dissimilar ACM. Two T-38/F-5 aircraft against F-4s, F-100s, A-7, F-15, or whatever happens to be available. All of the above are based on American tactics. When the student has demonstrated that he has a thorough knowledge of American tactics, he moves to: 5. Enemy Basic Fighter Maneuvers, which consists of learning to fly and maneuver like enemy formations. 6. Enemy Air Combat Maneuvering, which consists of a set up of two T-38s versus two dissimilar adversaries, a visual intercept and attack by the T-38s, using enemy tactics. 7. Enemy Air Combat Tactics, wherein ground-controlled intercept procedures are used to direct the T-38s against dissimilar aircraft. 8. Academics, which lean heavily towards an in-depth study of the enemy fighter pilot, his equipment, his philosophy, and his tactics. The potential Aggressor pilot is tested constantly throughout the check-out phase, and will not advance to the next area of training until his instructors are satisfied that he is competent in the current area. A great deal of stress is placed on the Aggressor's ability to use the tape recorder and chalk, for it is the debrief after a mission that determines the ultimate success or failure of the mission. Actual flying time for each sortie is usually less than an hour. Pre-brief and debrief sessions run two to three hours.

There are two squadrons of Aggressors in the United States, one in England, and one in the Phillipines. The Aggressors send detachments to each base within their command area to give realistic air combat training to TAC's aircrews. The curriculum for this training is determined by the individual unit's training officer. (Units with a primary air-to-air mission may want more advanced training, while the air-to-ground units may be more in need of the fundamentals.) In addition to the normal maintenance personnel, the Aggressors also have their own controllers. (Enemy fighter units depend heavily on ground control of their fighters.)

The Aggressor program has radically altered the face of American fighter training. If another war comes along, the American fighter pilot will start out with the advantage of familiarity with the enemy. If our intelligence community does its job, there won't be so many surprises . . . the Agressors will see to that!

F-5E of 425th TFTS, 58th TFTW, Williams AFB, AZ carries bright yellow bands edged in black on wings, fuselage, and vertical fin in attempt to make the small fighter more visible during training missions. (Charles B. Mayer)

F-5A of the 425th TFTS, which was then (1970) attached to the 4410th CCTW. Note refueling boom. Standard USAF camouflage. (Jerry Geer)

F-5/T-38 Specs:

Built by: Northrop Corporation. **F-5E Specs:** two GE J85-GE-21 engines of 5,000 lb. thrust each with afterburning. Single seat VFR day/night fighter, limited all-weather capability. Originally developed for use in MAP, providing allies with relatively inexpensive air superiority fighter. **Dimensions:** Span 26' 8", length 48'2", weights: empty 9,853 lb. max gross: 24,675 lb. **Performance:** at 13,220 lb: max level speed at 36,000 feet Mach 1.57, service ceiling 52,000 feet, range with max fuel, with reserve fuel for 20 min max endurance at sea level, (external tanks retained) 1,595 miles. **Armament:** two AIM-9 Sidewinders, two M-39A2 20mm cannon, with 280 rpg, 7,000 lbs. ordnance on four underwing hardpoints, and one centerline station. Capable of carrying AGM-65 Maverick missle or laser-guided bombs. Two seat F-5F version has similar performance specs and is equipped with laser-designator. **T-38 Specs:** Two seat trainer in continuous production from 1956 until 1972 has maintained best safety record of any USAF supersonic aircraft. Two GE J-85-GE-5 with 3,850 lbs. thrust with afterburning. **Dimensions:** Span 25' 3", length 46' 4½", weights: 7,164 lb. empty, 12,093 lb. gross. **Performance:** max speed at 36,000 feet Mach 1.23, service ceiling 55,000 feet, range 1,093 miles with reserve.

F-4E of 35th TFW, George AFB. (Jerry Geer)

F-4E/F of 35th TFW in Luftwaffe camouflage. 35th TFW provided initial training for Luftwaffe F-4 aircrew. (Don Logan)

Latest version of the F-4 equips 4th TFW, which has a primary air-to-air mission. (USAF)

F-4 Specs:

Over 650 F-4s are in TAC inventory, including F-4C, D, E, and G versions. USAFE has over 450 F-4s. Produced by McDonnell Douglas, the Phantom II has been in continuous production since 1958, and has proven a durable fighter by its adaptability to new weapons and avionics. **Dimensions:** Span 38' 5", length 62' 10", height 16' 3". Two GE J79-GE-17 engines of 17,900 lbs. thrust with afterburning. Weights: 30,425 lb. max. gross 58,000 lb. **Performance:** (F-4E) max speed at 40,000 feet mach 2.27 range with typical tactical load 1,300 miles. **Armament:** One 20mm M-61A-1 vulcan cannon, provision for up to four AIM-7 and four AIM-9 missiles, or up to 16,000 lbs. of external stores. Latest version of J-79 engines are smokeless, eliminating one of the biggest tactical disadvantages of the Phantom.

F-4E with latest version of the Sidewinder Missile, the AIM-9J, which has increased range and maneuvering capability. AIM-9J is being produced by Ford Aerospace by modification of existing stocks of AIM-9Bs. (USAF)

F-4E of 71st TFS, 1st TFW, MacDill AFB, 1972. (Norman E. Taylor)

F-4E of 335th TFS, 4th TFW, Seymour Johnson AFB, 1971. Equipped with 370 gal. wing tanks on outboard wing stations and baggage carrying pods on inboard stations for visit to Kelly AFB, Texas. (Norman E. Taylor)

F-4D of USAFE approaches KC-97L tanker of Illinois ANG over Germany in Summer 1976. F-4 is primary fighter of USAFE. (Lou Drendel)

35th TFW shield adorns side of F-4E at George AFB, California. (Norman E. Taylor)

F-4Es of 36th TFW line up for formation takeoff from Bitburg AB, Germany. (USAF)

32nd TFS operates late model version of the F-4E, with slatted wing and TISEO, from Camp New Amsterdam, Netherlands. (USAF)

F-4E equipped with 370 gallon wing tanks and 600 gallon centerline tank taxies through foggy Netherlands morning prior to training mission. (USAF)

Vulcan cannon pod-armed F-4D taxies in after a mission on Zaragoza AB's ranges, controlled by 406th TFTW. (USAFE)

32nd TFS groundcrewperson pulling maintenance on one of unit's F-4s. (USAF)

Practice Sidewinder-armed F-4Ds of 81st TFW pull their gear during formation takeoff from RAF Bentwaters. (USAFE)

32nd TSF personnel demonstrate weapons loading with AIM-9J Sidewinder, which weighs in at a hefty 159 lbs., making teamwork in this exercise essential. (USAFE)

Slatted F-4E of the 32nd TFS shows off full complement of F-4 air to air weaponry, including long range (14 miles) AIM-7 Sparrows, short range (2 miles) Sidewinder, and nose mounted cannon. (USAFE)

Captains Al Jackson and Mac Hornbaker scramble aboard F-4C of 18th TFW, loaded with AIM-7, AIM-9, and Vulcan cannon pod (on fuselage centerline). PACAF alert squadrons keep their F-4s ready to go in blast-proof shelters. (USAF)

F-4Es of 36th TFS, Osan AB, Korea take off from Yokota AB, Japan. All 8th TFW aircraft now carry tail code "UK". (Shinichi Ohtaki, Aviation Journal)

Phantoms of 44th and 25th TFS, 18th TFW approach Kadena AB for landing, 1977. 25th TFS Phantom carries 25th squadron emblem on intake, PACAF emblem on vertical fin. It also mounts a GE ALQ-87 ECM pod in right forward AIM-7 missile well, while the 44th F-4 carries an ALQ-119 pod on the same station. (Takeaki Hoshina via Aviation Journal)

F-4E belonging to squadron commander of 36th TFS, 8th TFW taxies at Yokota AB in 1975. Note unique application of serial number on tail, emphasizing the squadron number. (Shinichi Ohtaki via Norman E. Taylor)

(Above) F-15A Eagle of 58th TFTW at Luke AFB, AZ, Summer 1977. External fuel tank on centerline may also be carried on either wing hard point. (Scott Brown)

(Below) TF-15A of 58th TFTW in now-standard two tone Grey camouflage. Air Superiority Blue camouflage applied to first F-15s proved highly visible in the air and was abandoned in favor of low reflectivity Greys. (Scott Brown)

F-15 Specs:

Built by McDonnell Douglas and designed from the ground up as a pure Air Superiority Machine, the Eagle holds several time-to-climb altitude records, made possible by the excess thrust provided by its twin P&W F-100-PW-100 afterburning turbofans, which put out 25,000 lbs. thrust each. USAF plans a total procurement of 729 Eagles. **Dimensions:** Span 42' 9", length 63' 9" height 18' 5½". **Performance:** max speed mach 2.5, combat ceiling 65,000 feet, ferry range, without Fast Packs, more than 2,878 miles. (Fast Packs, capable of carrying 10,000 lbs of fuel each can be fitted to fuselage sides. Since they are streamlined, they offer no subsonic drag penalty. They can also be fitted with a variety of reconnaissance, ECM, or weapons, giving the Eagle even more versatility.) **Armament:** one M-61A1 20mm cannon mounted in starboard wing fairing, four AIM-7 Sparrow Missiles on fuselage, four AIM-9 Sidewinder missiles on wing stations. Also provision for up to 15,000 lbs ordnance on three hardpoints. Weapons system has HUD (Heads-Up-Display) which allows pilot to operate all aspects of the weapons system without looking in cockpit when he is within ten miles of his target. (All switches are either on throttle or stick)

TF-15A shows off its massive speed brake as it taxies. Eagle was designed for maintainability and requires fewer maintenance man hours between flights than the P-51 did in World War II! (Charles B. Mayer)

(Above) F-15A of 461st TFTS, 58th TFTW, Luke AFB, AZ, with "fake" canopy applied to bottom of fuselage under the real thing. USAF experimented with this on several different types of aircraft, reasoning that in tight-turning aerial combat, the enemy could be deceived into thinking that you were turning into him when you were really turning away from him. (Charles B. Mayer)

(Below) F-15A of 58th TFTW in high-visibility markings of red and white stripes on wings and fuselage. F-15 stabilators, vertical fins and rudders, and engines are identical and interchangeable from left to right side of aircraft, making for smaller spares inventories. (A. Swanberg via Jerry Geer)

(Above) F-15A of 1st TFW at Langley AFB, VA, Summer 1977. Eagle's gun is permanently boresighted and can be replaced without need of test firing for accuracy. F-15 also carried complete built-in self test capacity for all systems, most of which are accessible without ladders or maintenance stands, through 570 square feet of access panels and doors. (K. Fujita, Aviation Journal)

(Left) F-15A of 58th TFTW with black bordered yellow bands on wings and tail. F-15 has no leading edge devices on wings, and simple two position flaps. Large wing area offers superior maneuverability and is effective for aerodynamic braking on landing, precluding necessity for drag chute. (A. Swanberg via Jerry Geer)

(Below) F-15s of 1st TFW at Langley AFB, VA. Also visible with the BT tailcode are F-15s of 36th TFW, first USAFE unit to operate the Eagle. 36th's F-15 staged out of Langley enroute to Europe in Summer 1977. (USAF photo by SMSGT Bob Kapperman)

58th TFTW Eagles in experimental three-tone splinter camouflage patterns which are most graphic evidence of Air Force's renewed interest in developing effective air superiority tactics and equipment. (Scott Brown)

F-16 Specs:

Lightweight Fighter program was begun in 1972 in an effort to procure a relatively inexpensive, highly effective air superiority fighter. General Dynamics won the competition and was awarded a contract for six full size (production version is 10 inches longer and has increased wing area) F-16A and two F-16B two place development aircraft. Innovations include a fly-by-wire control system, with control inputs through a side-mounted control stick, 30 degree reclined seat which allows pilot to withstand more Gs, single piece bubble canopy for increased visibility, blended wing-body aerodynamics with forebody strakes and automatically variable wing leading edges to enhance maneuverability. F-16 uses the same Pratt & Whitney F-100 engine that powers the F-15 Eagle. USAF plans to acquire 650 F-16s, and NATO countries of Belgium, Denmark, Norway, and Netherlands will procure 348 F-16s. **Dimensions:** Span 32' 10", length 49' 6", height 16' 6". Weights: empty 15,000 lb. max gross 33,000 lb. **Performance:** max speed Mach 2+, ferry range more than 2,200 miles. **Armament:** one M-61A1 20mm cannon with 500 rounds. AIM-9 missle on each wingtip, also provision for air to ground stores on underwing hardpoints.

First prototype of the F-16 Lightweight Fighter which will enter USAF service in 1979. It is illustrated with 370 gallon wing tanks and Sidewinder AAMs on wingtip launchers. (General Dynamics)

F-104G of 58th TFTW at Luke AFB, AZ, with practice bomb dispenser on centerline. 58th trains pilots for West German Luftwaffe, which uses its 104s for air-to-ground missions. (Doug Slowiak via Paul Stevens)

TF-104G at Nellis AFB, Nevada (Don Logan)

F-104D of USAF. Starfighter was the original lightweight fighter. Its amazing performance was never fully exploited while it served with active USAF combat squadrons. (USAF)

F-104 Specs:

F-104G: **Dimensions:** Span 21' 11", length 54' 9", height 13' 6". Empty Weight 14,082 lb. Max TO Weight 28,799 lb. **Performance:** Max level speed at 36,000 feet mach 2.2 = 1,450 mph. Rate of climb at sea level 50,000 feet per minut. Service ceiling 58,000 feet, but has been zoomed to over 90,000 feet. Radius with max fuel 745 miles.

AIR INTERDICTION

TAC's advertised definition of Air Interdiction is: "action taken to destroy enemy ground and naval forces before they can be brought to bear against friendly forces by denying the enemy's deployed combat forces the supplies, mobility, and reinforcements needed to carry out sustained operations." Air Interdiction as it is thus defined achieved dramatic results and became a permanent part of modern warfare in the last year of World War II, when Allied fighter-bombers roamed the skies of Europe disrupting German logistics. The Korean War proved that jet aircraft could perform the interdiction mission too, as F-80 and F-84 fighter-bombers devasted the North Korean supply lines, forcing the enemy to move his troops and material by night and hide them by day.

The Vietnam War, because of its length and complexity, provided opportunity for new and imaginative methods of interdiction. In the early phase of the war, the Communists used small and mobile bands of guerillas, whose only readily definable lines of supply were in North Vietnam or down the Ho Chi Minh Trail. Since the majority of the Ho Chi Minh Trail ran through the neutral countries of Laos and Cambodia, it was technically off-limits to interdiction strikes. The bulk of tactical interdiction missions were flown against the source of supply in North Vietnam, with tactical fighters going against what would have been considered strategic targets in most other conflicts. Ironically, SAC's bomber force was relegated to flying missions against tactical targets in South Vietnam since it was felt that the B-52 could not survive the increasingly deadly air defense system over the North. That air defense environment fostered the development of a whole new generation of penetration aids and weapons. The penetration aids are covered in the electronic warfare section of this book. The new weapons developed have been popularly classified as "smart" bombs. A great deal of the losses incurred by tactical air in Vietnam were as a direct result of having to go back to a given target after the enemy had been forewarned and given the chance to stiffen his air defenses around the target. The new weapons were developed to give tactical air the ability to take out a target on the first try, negating the necessity to return to the same target day after day.

As the North Vietnamese gradually began to shift tactics to the employment of large units in set-piece battles, interdiction of their entire supply line took on new importance. The charade of impunity for the Ho Chi Minh trail was dropped, and the Communists were forced to move only at night. USAF tac air responded with C-130 FAC's equipped with night vision devices capable of spotting enemy trucks and directing the bombers onto the targets. The C-130 was modified into one of the most devastating weapons in aerial warfare as the gunship came of age, and the AC-130 became the scourge of the Ho Chi Minh trail. Technically assigned to the Special Operations Force, the Gunships are one of the most effective interdiction weapons in TAC's inventory.

Aerial interdiction of North Vietnamese supply lines and weapons stockpiles defeated the North's 1972 bid to take South Vietnam. It took the North two years to recover from the destruction wrought by tac air. When they tried again USAF tac air was not there to stop them, and there is no longer a South Vietnam. There can be no more obvious an example of the necessity for effective tactical air interdiction in today's Air Force.

F-4E of the 388th TFW in its revetment at Korat RTAB, November 1970. It is loaded with CBUs and 500 lb. bombs for interdiction of North Vietnamese supply lines through Laos. (USAF)

17

(Above) F-4D of 432nd TRW taking off from Udorn RTAB during October 1972 Linebacker campaign against North Vietnam. (USAF)

(Right) Nighttime maintenance of 18th TFW F-4s at Kadena AB. (USAF by Capt. Mac Hornbaker)

(Below) F-4D of 8th TFS, 49th TFW landing at Elmendorf AFB, Alaska, during 1969 exercise "Punch Card VII". Inscription on intake reads; "Catch me if you can!" (Norman E. Taylor)

F-4E of 57th FWW, USAF TFWC, Nellis, AFB loaded with ALQ-119 ECM pod and AGM-65 Maverick TV guided missile. (USAF)

355th TFW F-105D loaded for 1970 mission against Communist supply lines from Takhli RTAB. Thud's great low-level performance made it a favorite for armed reconnaissance missions during this period. (Col. Don Kutyna)

"The Underdog", a 44th TFS Thud taxies out for a 1970 mission. Four of the eight 500 lb. bombs it carries have fuse extenders, which will ensure that the bombs explode before burying themselves in the ground, making them more effective anti-personnel weapons. (Col Don Kutyna)

"The Polish Glider", Don Kutyna's airplane, enroute to target, loaded with 750 lb and 500 lb bombs. (USAF via Don Kutyna)

F-105 Specs:

F-105 first flew in 1955. A total of 833 were built, including the three basic versions, B, D, & F. ANG and AFRES have several squadrons, including 30 of the modified T-Stick II Ds, which have improved all-weather bombing capability. Two Squadrons of the regular Air Force fly the F-105G Wild Weasel two seat version. Built by Fairchild Republic, the last Thud rolled off the assembly line in 1964. Powered by one P&W J75-P-19W engine of 26,500 lb thrust with afterburning and water injection. **Dimensions:** Span 34' 11½", length 67', height 19' 8". Weights: 27,500 lb empty, 52,545 lb max gross. **Performance:** max speed at 38,000 feet mach 2.1, service ceiling 52,000 feet, max range over 1,842 miles. **Armament:** one M61-A1 20mm cannon in nose, with capability to carry over 14,000 lb of stores under wings and fuselage.

(Above) "Billie Fern" and "High Stepper" of the 354th TFS, 355th TFW enroute to targets in 1970. F-105D has NASARR monopulse radar system, for use in both high and low-level missions, and Doppler for night or nasty weather missions. (USAF)

(Below) 355th TFW Thuds on the tanker during a mission against Communist targets in Vietnam. During armed recce missions, Thuds often tanked more than once, using their ordnance as required for several different targets in widely scattered areas of operations. (USAF)

Thud with T-Stick II conversion easily identifiable by its avionics "humpback". 523rd TFS, 23rd TFW, McConnell AFB, April 1971. (Jerry Geer)

F-105D of 563rd TFS, 23rd TFW at McConnell in November 1970. (Jerry Geer)

F-111 Specs:

The F-111 was built by General Dynamics. (Production ended in 1976) It was the center of controversy during its early test and operational life, but has proven to be the best all-weather penetration attack aircraft ever built. It was built in seven different versions, of which five are operated by TAC. The F-111A is the basic version, and is operated by the 474th TFW. It was superceded on the production line by the E model, which is flown by the 20th TFW. The 27th TFW flys the D version, the 366th TFW flys the F version, and the EF-111 will equip as yet unspecified ECM units of TAC. Power Plant are; F-111A/E: two P&W TF-30-P-3 turbofans of 18,500 lb thurst each with afterburning. F-111D: two TF-30-P-100 of 25,100 lb each with afterburning. Two man crew, side by side seating (Pilot and WSO) in escape module. **Dimensions:** Span 63' spread, 31' 11" swept, length 73' 6", height 17' 1". Weights (F-111A) 46,172 lb empty, 91,500 lb max gross. **Performance:** (F-111A) max speed at sea level mach 1.2, max speed at altitude mach 2.2, service ceiling 51,000 feet, range max internal fuel 3,165 miles. **Armament:** one 20mm M61-A1 cannon or two 750 lb bombs in internal weapons bay; four swiveling and four fixed wing pylons carrying total external load of up to 25,000 lb of ordnance or fuel.

(Above) F-111D of the 27th TFW, Cannon AFB, N.M. The 27th has operated the F-111 since 1969, the late model D version since 1971. (D.W. Menard via Norman E. Taylor)

F-111 refueling from KC-97 of Texas ANG. The swing-wing design of the 111 gives it the capability to refuel from slower aircraft, such as the KC-97 without the startling angles of attack demonstrated by some other modern fighters, which appear to be hanging on for dear life. (USAF via Norman E. Taylor)

F-111s of the 77th TFS, 20th TFW, refuel over Europe during a 1971 mission. (USAF)

F-111E of the 77th TFS, 20th TFW, RAF Upper Heyford, England as it appeared in 1971. Pylons under wings swing with the wings to maintain their position relative to centerline of aircraft. (Normal E. Taylor)

(Above) F-111E of the 20th TFW. Side by side seating of the 111 is an advantage for crew communications and coordination, but the penalty is a relatively large frontal area. (USAF)

(Below) 20th TFW ground crew install weapons pylon on wing of F-111E. (USAF)

(Above) 20th TFW 111 being directed to parking spot at RAF Upper Heyford. Aardvark on back of T-shirt is symbolic of unofficial name of the F-111. USAF has never officially nick-named the F-111, probably due to the storm of adverse publicity given the airplane. (USAF)

(Below) F-111D of 27th TFW. F-111s inertial navigation system and terrain-following-radar make it the best bet to penetrate highly sophisticated air defense environments in foul weather. (Charles B. Mayer)

B-57E on final approach to Shaw AFB, SC in 1970. The English Electric designed and built Canberra was license built in U.S. by the Martin Company. Its stability as a weapons delivery platform made it a popular night interdiction bomber in Vietnam. (Jim Sullivan)

B-57G of the 4424th CCTW, 1st TFW in 1972. 16 B-57Gs were remanufactured from B models. Equipped with the latest radar, infrared sensors and laser range-finding equipment, they flew night interdiction missions with the 13th TBS, out of Ubon AB against the Ho Chi Minh Trail for two (1970-72) years. (Jerry Geer)

CLOSE AIR SUPPORT

Close Air Support is defined as air-to-ground operations conducted in close integration with the fire and maneuver of friendly surface forces which are directly engaged with enemy forces in the immediate battle area.

At the beginning of the 70s, TAC had no pure close air support aircraft. The mission was being performed by the F-100, which had begun life as an air superiority fighter and was the glamor fighter of the fifties, now relegated to finishing its tour as a mud-mover because the skies of North Vietnam were considered non-survivable for the aging Supersabre. The job was also being done by the F-4, designed as an interceptor, now performing every imaginable fighter duty; the A-7, perhaps the best of the group because of its sophisticated weapons delivery system, but still not as nimble or as tough as the mission dictated an aircraft should be; the A-37, a converted trainer, the "Super Tweet" was a pleasant surprise, but not the complete answer, and finally, the A-1, still around after 25 years of service. The latter two are classified by TAC as "Special Operations" aircraft, but close air support is mostly what they did.

It was beginning to sound repetitious, but the close air support mission, like the air superiority mission, had fallen victim to the military malaise of commonality. During the battle for An Loc in 1972, the most effective tank killer was the TOW missile-equipped Army helicopter gunship. The Spring 1972 offensive against South Vietnam proved the need for an aircraft designed specifically for close air support . . . an aircraft capable of knocking out tanks . . . an aircraft capable of operating under low ceilings with poor visibility . . . an aircraft capable of hitting its targets with pin-point accuracy. Ironically, the airplane destined to win the AX competition made its first flight on 10 May 1972. The A-10, with its GAU-8 30mm cannon, 16,000 pounds of varied ordnance, wide radius of action with long loiter time, and survivability gives TAC the ultimate close air support machine.

One of the rare birds of TAC, the AT-33A of the 4430th CCTS, "Teeny Tigers", at Myrtle Beach AFB, SC, 1972. (Jim Sullivan)

F-100D of the 27th TFW, 524th TFS, shortly before that unit's conversion to the F-111 in late 1969. 27th's F-100s were turned over to ANG and AFRES units. (Jerry Geer)

F-100D of 309th TFS, 31st TFW, Tuy Hoa AB, Vietnam, 1970. F-100 was the premier USAF close support aircraft in South Vietnam throughout much of the war. (USAF)

"Thor's Hammer", F-100D of the 309th TFS in the arming pit at Tuy Hoa getting its guns safed after a mission. (USAF)

F-100 Specs:

Built by North American, The F-100 Supersabre was the successor to the F-86, and was the first operational fighter in the world to exceed the speed of sound in level flight. Production lines closed in 1959, but the "Hun" continues to soldier on in USAF ANG. During its long and distinguished career, the F-100 performed in the role of air superiority, nuclear strike, fast FAC, and finally, close support fighter. **Dimensions:** Span 38' 9", length 47', height 15' weights: empty 21,000 lb, gross 34,832 lb. **Performance:** (F-100D) powered by one P&W J57-P-21A of 17,000 lb thrust with afterburner. Max speed at 36,000 feet mach 1.3, range with two external tanks, 1,500 miles. **Armament:** four 20mm M39E cannon in nose; underwing pylons for six 1,000 lb bombs, two Sidewinder or Bullpup missiles, rockets, or other ordnance.

B-57G of 4424th CCTS, 1st TFW.

EB-66B of the 39th TEWTS, Shaw AFB, SC, 1970

A-26s flew night interdiction missions against Ho Chi Minh trail from Nakhon Phanom AB, Thailand, 1970

C-130E of the 345th TAS, 314th TAW, Vietnam, 1970

A-37B of the 8th SOS, 14th SOW, Bien Hoa AB, Vietnam, 1970. Though officially christened the "Dragonfly", the A-37 was more familiarly known as the "Super Tweet", a legacy of the unofficial name for its more docile sire, the T-37 "Tweety Bird". (Norman E. Taylor)

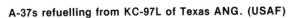

A-37s refuelling from KC-97L of Texas ANG. (USAF)

(Above Right) A-37B of the 427th SOS, 4410th CCTW at McConnell AFB for 1971 airshow. The A-37 was developed during the surge of active interest in Counterinsurgency warfare. 39 A-37As were built, 511 A-37Bs following off Cessna assembly lines. Only USAF units now equipped with the A-37 are the 434th TFW, AFRES, and the 175th TFG, and the 174th TFG, ANG. A-37s have played an active role in Military Assistance Programs. (Jerry Geer)

A-37B of 8th SOS has just released a pair of 500 lb "Snakeye" high drag bombs on a VC target. The A-37 proved itself an able performer in the close air support role, and saw service right up the bitter end of the Vietnam War. (USAF via Norman E. Taylor)

A-37B of 603rd SOS, 1st SOW, Hurlburt Field, Florida, 1970. A-37B is capable of carrying more than its empty weight (6,200 lb) in fuel and stores over a 460 mile range. (Norman E. Taylor)

A-1H of the 56th SOW flew RESCAP missions out of Nakhon Phanom AB, Thailand. The A-1 was hardly ever called by its official name of "Skyraider". To the Navy, for whom it was designed, it became the "Spad". To the USAF it became the "Sandy", because that was the call sign of the RESCAP forces, and the A-1 became synonomous with that mission. (USAF)

"Miss Judy" starting its engine prior to mission from Nakhon Phanom in 1972. The RESCAP mission is an exacting form of close air support, and the pilots who flew these missions had the responsibility to keep enemy guns "down" while the Jolly Green Giant helicopters dashed in to snatch downed pilots. (USAF)

EB-66E of the 39th
TEWTS, Shaw AFB, SC,
June 1972. (Norman E.
Taylor)

F-100D of the 612th TFS loaded with firebombs for close
air support mission, Vietnam,
1971

F-5B of the 425th TFTS, 58th
TFTW, Williams AFB, Arizona

Cessna 0-2A of the 21st TASS,
Phu Cat AB, Vietnam, 1970.

AC-119K Gunship 1st SOW, Hurlburt Field, Fla. 1972

A-1 Skyraider flew escort missions for Jolly Green rescue helicopters from Nakhon Pha-non AB, Thailand

RF-4C of 91st TRS, 67th TFW, Bergstrom AFB, Texas, 1973. (Norman E. Taylor)

CH-3E of 317th SOS, 1st SOW Hurlburt Field, Fla. 1973

F-4D of 49th TFW, Hol-loman AFB, N.M., 1974. (Jim Sullivan)

A-7D of the 355th TFW, Davis Monthan AFB, AZ, 1973. The A-7D, known to the Navy as the "Corsair II", was dubbed "SLUF" by USAF pilots (Short Little Ugly F---fill in your own blanks). It was the first of the new generation of aircraft designed with the maintenance man in mind. (Note that most access panels are within easy reach without the use of ladders or stands.) First deliveries of the A-7D were made in December 1968. (Jerry Geer)

A-7s from 57th FWW carry 500 lb bombs and napalm during ordnance delivery training at Nellis AFB. (LTV)

A-7D Specs:

Built by the Vought Corporation, subsidiary of LTV Corporation, the A-7D is the USAF version of the A-7 series for the U.S. Navy. It is powered by the Allison TF41-A-1 non-afterburning Turbofan engine of 14,250 lb thrust. It is a single seater and carries a computerized navigation/weapon delivery system providing automatic moding, accurate self-contained navigation, terrain following during navigation, multimode attack capability, target cueing, head-up operation, unconstrained attack profiles, and automatic, accurate weapons release. **Dimensions:** Span 38' 9", length 46' 1'' height 16' Weights: empty 19,781 lb. **Performance:** Max speed at sea level 698 mph, ferry range with external tanks 2,871 miles. **Armament:** one M61-A-1 20mm cannon, up to 15,000 lbs of air-to-air or air-to-ground ordnance on six underwing pylons and two fuselage attachment points.

A-7s in echelon over the Nevada dessert. SLUF's main claim to fame lies in its extraordinary accuracy in dropping dumb bombs, using its continuous-solution navigation and weapons delivery system. (LTV)

A-7D of the 3rd TFS. The SLUF achieved such no-teriety for its accurate delivery of bombs that it was assigned the role of RESCAP during the late stages of USAF involvement in Vietnam. (LTV)

(Above) A-7D of the 355th TFW, Davis Monthan AFB, AZ, 1974 in experimental camouflage of dark blue-gray overall. (Ben Kowles via Norman E. Taylor)

(Below) A-7D of 355th TFS, 354th TFW, Myrtle Beach AFB, SC in 1971 prior to that unit's departure for Korat RTAFB, where it blooded the A-7D in battle for the first time. (Norman E. Taylor)

F-111A enroute to strike targets in North Vietnam during Linebacker operation in 1972. F-111s flew alone at night, in all weather, at low altitude, using their TFR systems.

Thunderbirds 1975 demonstration, as seen from rear cockpit of slot (Number 4) aircraft. (USAF)

KC-97L of Illinois Air Guard at Rhein-Main, Germany during 1976 Creek Party deployment. (Lou Drendel)

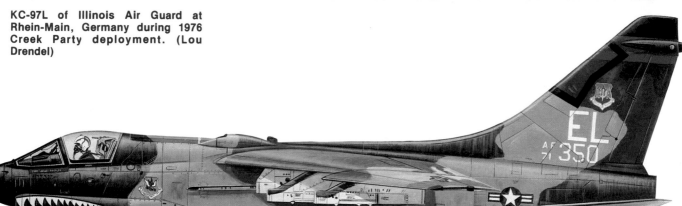

A-7D Corsair II of the 23rd TFW "Flying Tigers", England AFB, Louisiana 1976.

A-37B of 4406th CCTW, England AFB, La.

Fairchild Republic A-10A, the close air support aircraft of the future. (Charles B. Mayer)

A-10A's 30mm GAU-8/A multibarrel tank killing cannon is exposed by opening access panels under nose. Effectiveness of the GAU-8/A is illustrated by sequence of photos at left which depict the destruction of M-48 tank with one short burst. A-10A's cannon has also been successfully tested against Soviet T-62 tank captured by the Israelis in 1973 war. (USAF)

AGM-65 Maverick TV guided "smart" bomb is wheeled to waiting A-10A during testing. The A-10 can carry up to six Mavericks, in addition to its other ordnance. (USAF)

355th TFW ground crew and pilot confer prior to A-10 test flight from Davis Monthan AFB. (USAF)

A-10A Specs:

A-10A is the winner of AX competition to design and build an aircraft specifically for the close air support mission. (Northrop A-9A was the loser.) First production aircraft flew in October 1975, and 355th TFTW began A-10A operations in March 1976. A-10s outstanding design features include capability to carry large loads of diverse ordnance over long range, loiter in target area with the maneuvering capability and armor to survive tough air defense environments, deliver weapons with great accuracy and return to base for quick turn-around missions. Two prototypes, six pre-production, and 195 production A-10s have been funded to date, with a further 144 requested in FY78 budget. First operational squadron was activated at Myrtle Beach AFB, SC in July 1977. Two General Electric TF34-GE-100 turbofans with 9,065 lbs. thrust each. **Dimensions:** Span 57' 6", length 53' 4", height 14' 8". Weight: max gross 47,400 lb. **Performance:** combat speed at sea level tropic day, clean 423 mph, range with 9,500 lb ordnance and two hour loiter, 20 minute reserve, 288 miles. **Armament:** one 30mm GAU-8/A cannon in nose, eight underwing hard points and three under fuselage for up to 16,000 lbs ordnance, including various types of free-fall or guided bombs, gun pods, or 6 AGM-65 AGMs, and chaff or other jamming pods.

Number 5 A-10A enroute from Edwards AFB to Nellis AFB range with Rockeye anti-tank weapons and Maverick AGMs during weapons testing phase of A-10A flight test program. (USAF)

A-10A of 333rd TFTS, 355th TFTW, Davis Monthan AFB, AZ. After trial of several different camouflage schemes, the Air Force has settled on a two tone low reflectivity grey paint scheme which will degrade the radar signature of the A-10. In modern air combat, the eyeball has been supplanted by radar and those striking multi-colored camouflage schemes may be gone forever. (Charles B. Mayer)

RF-4C on a low level reconnaissance of North Vietnamese AAA positions.

Four standard camouflage schemes used on USAF Aggressor
aircraft (T-38 and F-5). Of the four, the grey scheme is most
effective for air-to-air (hardest to see). These aircraft belong to 64th
and 65th Fighter Weapons Squadrons, Nellis AFB, Nevada. Other
Aggressor outfits may use variations on these colors and patterns.
(Lou Drendel)

T-38A in "Ghost" grey camouflage belongs to 65th Fighter
Weapons Squadron "Aggres-
sors"

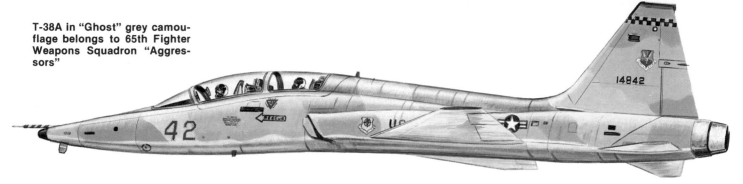

F-4C of the 58th TFTW sporting high visibility markings used in training. (Scott Brown)

F-15A Eagle of 58th TFTW in three tone gray camouflage. Note fake canopy painted on underside of nose. (Scott Brown)

F-15A in the now standard two-tone gray. It is interesting to note that all current USAF camouflage schemes, standard or experimental, use some variation of gray, making it certain that it will be the air superiority camouflage color of the future. (Scott Brown)

TF-15A Eagle of the 58th TFTW, Luke AFB, Arizona.

SPECIAL OPERATIONS FORCE

If the name fails to evoke an instant mental picture of the aircraft or actions of this diverse and unique unit, it is not because they lack color. In fact, SOF is among the more colorful, if sometimes secrecy-shrouded, units in the Tactical Air Forces. They trace their lineage back to the Air Commandos of World War II, who fought with ingenuity and cunning in the China-Burma-India Theater. The Air Commandos of World War II were disbanded in 1948, a casualty of nuclear strategic thinking, and the hope that the United States would never have to fight another war like that one.

Early in the 1960s, Tactical Air was making a comeback, and tactical strategists were beginning to take to heart the avowed Communist intention of world domination through "wars of liberation". To counter this threat, USAF activated the 4400th Combat Crew Training Squadron at Hurlburt Field, Florida in 1961. There was never any doubt about the training, and the operation that had been dubbed "Jungle Jim" produced the official name change by which the unit was to become more familiarly known as . . . The 1st Air Commando Group. A month after the name became official, President John F. Kennedy directed the armed forces to strengthen their ability to fight guerilla warfare, especially Communist "wars of liberation".

A year after this policy-changing message, the squadron that had expanded to a group was further expanded to a Wing. Its fortunes became inextricably bound to the war in Southeast Asia which was to be the ultimate test of U.S. Counterinsurgency policy. Ironically, the Air Commando name, as well as the Special Air Warfare Center tag for Hurlburt Field were changed in 1968 to the more innocuous sounding (for public relations reasons, I suspect) Special Operations Force, before the only true large scale commando raid of the war was carried out. The raid on the North Vietnamese prison camp at Son Tay, in November 1971, was a magnificently planned and executed example of joint Army-Air Force special operations.

Throughout the decade of the 70s, the basic mission of the 1st SOW has remained unchanged. As the focal point for Air Force special operations, the wing has more sophisticated capabilities than the original air commandos. Its missions include assisting in the internal defense of allied nations, conducting psychological operations, managing unconventional warfare assets and related activities, including the training of friendly forces to defend against guerilla forces.

AC-47 Specs:

Engines: 2 P&W R-1830-90D radials of 1,200 hp each. **Dimensions:** Span 95', length 64' 4", height 16' 10". **Performance:** Speed 230 mph, Ceiling 24,900 feet. Weight 29,000 lb. loaded. **Armament:** three 7.62mm miniguns, capable of firing up to 6,000 rpm.

Lineup of SOF aircraft in early 70s gives testament to the diverse roles assigned to Special Operations. (USAF)

C-130E Combat Talon Blackbird, so named because of its green and black camouflage and its mission. It is equipped with The Fulton Recovery System and specialized aerial delivery equipment.

The most venerable aircraft to see action with TAC in the 70s was the C-47, which first flew in the 1930s. In its gunship version, the AC-47 "Spooky" (also known as "Puff, The Magic Dragon") mounts three 7.62 mm six-barrel miniguns, capable of 6,000 rounds per minute rate of fire. It was used extensively in Vietnam for night close air support of isolated ARVN outposts, a mission for which it was ideally suited. It had long loiter times, was able to carry enough ammunition and flares to stay on station several hours, and proved a stable gun platform. (USAF)

GUNSHIPS

Though the idea for heavily armed aircraft is nothing new, (witness the 75mm cannon equipped B-25 of WWII) the armament and application of transport aircraft to the night interdiction and close air support mission is a new and typically ingenious wrinkle in TAC's quest for new ways to accomplish old missions. Credit for bringing the gunship idea to fruition belongs to Ralph Flexman, an assistant chief engineer for Bell Aerosystems and a Major in the Air Force Reserves in the early 60s, and Lt. Col. Gilmour C. MacDonald, an inventor who had first proposed the idea during World War II for Anti-submarine patrol aircraft. World War II ended before MacDonald's idea could be tested, and it languished until a chance meeting between Flexman and MacDonald at Eglin AFB. Flexman had read about a method for delivering mail by bush pilots in South America whereby the pilot flew a pylon turn about a clearing while lowering a weighted pouch. If the turn were flown precisely, the pouch would remain in the same relative position in the clearing, and person on the ground could retrieve mail or supplies from it and insert outgoing mail. The pilot then hauled the pouch in and proceeded to his next delivery. Flexman reasoned that if a pouch on the end of a rope could be kept in the same position with this method, then an aircraft firing machine guns out of its side windows should be able to concentrate its fire on one spot. The press for new counterinsurgency weapons in the early sixties resulted in trials of the idea. The first gunship was a modified C-131, and the first tests were conducted over Eglin's water ranges. They were more of a success than even Flexman and MacDonald had anticipated. Those tests, conducted in 1964, were the beginning of the gunship as we know it today.

AC-47 of the 1st SOW at Hurlburt Field, Florida in October 1974. Ironically, many a young TAC aircraft commander has had the distinction of flying an aircraft older than himself. (Bill Sides via Jim Sullivan)

20mm cannon and 7.62 mm miniguns sprout from side of AC-119. (Ken Buchanan)

(Above) AC-119K "Stinger" gunship. When the C-47 proved itself so adaptable to the gunship mission, the next logical progression was to the C-119, another veteran transport in search of a new lease on life. (USAF) (Below) AC-119Gs of 17th SOS stopped at Elmendorf AFB enroute to Vietnam in 1969. (Norman E. Taylor)

The number 3 F-16A production version of the Lightweight Fighter. TAC is scheduled to activate the first F-16 wing at Hill AFB, Utah in 1979

Production A-10A in two tone low reflectivity gray paint scheme which is current standard camouflage. (Charles B. Mayer)

A-10 Thunder . . .? Close Air Support aircraft of the future for TAC was introduced to the inventory of 355th TFW in 1977.

AC-119G of the 17th SOS at Phu Cat AB, Vietnam, September, 1970. This model of the "Flying Boxcar" was dubbed "Shadow", and 53-3178 carried that name under cockpit. (Norman E. Taylor)

AC-119G 52-5892 of the 17th SOS was named "Charlie Chasers". It flew out of Phu Cat in 1970. (Norman E. Taylor)

AC-119 Specs:

The C-119 Flying Boxcar was an outgrowth of the C-82 Packet, and first flew in 1947. It served with distinction in the Korean War as a troop transport, and was used in the two combat jumps made by the 187th AIR. It was the standard delivery aircraft for airborne troops and equipment throughout the fifties. A total of 1,112 were built by Fairchild for USAF and countries in MAP. 52 C-119s were modified to the gunship configuration, 26 as C-119Gs and 26 as C-119Ks. Principle difference in the two gunship versions is the addition of two J-85 jet engines to the K version which gave it improved performance and additional payload. The K also added forward-looking infra-red sensor, side and forward looking radar and additional avionics. **Weights:** empty 58,282 lb, gross 80,400 lb. **Performance:** max level speed 250 mph at 10,000 feet, service ceiling (one engine out) 23,500 ft. range with max payload 1,980 miles. **Armament:** four GE SUU-11 gun pods, each containing a 7.62mm minigun, and (AC-119K only) two 20mm M61A-1 guns.

AC-119K at Hurlburt Field, Florida. Gunship crews are trained at Hurlburt. (USAF)

AC-119K of the 18th SOS flew out of Nakhon Phanom AB, Thailand in 1970-71. (Norman E. Taylor)

AC-130A at Hurlburt field, finished in overall dark blue-gray camouflage. AC-130 is the largest gunship flying. (Ken Buchanan)

Prototype AC-130 carried four 7.62 mm miniguns and four 20 mm M61A-1 cannon. It was initially called "Gunship II". (USAF)

AC-130 Specs:

The AC-130A/H were modified from basic Lockheed transport version by Greenville (Texas) Division of E-Systems, Inc. Initial versions were armed with four 7.62 mm miniguns, and four 20 mm M61A-1 cannon. They also carried forward-looking infrared target acquisition equipment and low-light-level TV and laser target designators, plus the computer to transmit all the data received by these systems into sighting information for the pilot. During attack, the pilot flies aileron only, with the aid of flight engineer who calls off degrees of bank. Co-pilot flies altitude and air-speed. Latest versions of the AC-130 carry 40 mm cannon and a 105 mm howitzer that recoils 3½ feet into fuselage when fired!

AC-130A "Spectre" derived its name from radio call sign of first unit to take the 130 gunship into combat. Inscription under nose art reads: "Mors De Caelis". (USAF via Norman E. Taylor)

AC-130A at Elmendorf AFB, Alaska enroute to Vietnam in 1968. (Norman E. Taylor)

AC-130E at Hurlburt. (Ken Buchanan)

AC-130E in its revetment in SE Asia awaits nightfall. Spectres became the scourge of the Ho Chi Minh Trail with their sophisticated avionics which enabled them to spot and kill NVA supply trucks moving down the trail at night. (USAF)

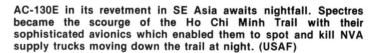

RC-130S Lightship on final for Shaw AFB. SC. Two C-130s were modified for search and rescue missions. They mount 28 highpowered lights, which put out 6.14 million candlepower. They were flown by the 446th TAW out of Ellington AFB, Texas. They are officially known as BIAS aircraft. (Battlefield Illumination Airborne System.) (Jim Sullivan)

CH-3E of the SOF at Hurlburt Field. (USAF)

HH-3E of 703rd TASS, 363rd TRW, Shaw AFB, SC. 1972. (Norman E. Taylor)

CH-3E of USAF Southern Air Division, Albrook AFB, Canal Zone. (USAF)

CH-3E Specs

Built by Sikorsky Aircraft Division, United Aircraft Corp., the CH-3 is powered by two GE T-58 GE-5 gas turbine engines, of 1,500 shp each. **Dimensions:** Length 72' 10", width 17' 4", height 18' 1". Rotor: 62'. **Performance:** max speed 142 knots, average cruise 110 knots, ceiling above 12,000 feet, range over 630 NM, max gross takeoff weight 22,050 lbs. It can carry 25 passengers, 16 litter patients or a 5,000 lb. payload. It is fully amphibious, all-weather instrument aircraft, and the forerunner of the HH-3E Jolly Green Giant which endeared itself to combat pilots who depended on the Jolly Green to be there if they went down.

HH-53 approaching for landing at Nellis AFB, Nevada, 1976. HH-53 was ordered in September 1966 specifically for USAF Aerospace Rescue and Recovery Service and became known as the "Super Jolly Green Giant." (Author)

HH-53 of the 81st TFW at Sembach AB, Germany. (USAF)

HH-53 Specs:

Built by Sikorsky Aircraft Division, United Aircraft Corp., HH-53 is larger and faster than the HH-3 which it was intended to supplant. It carries the same basic equipment as the HH-3. It is powered by two GE-64-GE-3 turboshaft engines of 3,080 shp each which give it a top speed of 186 mph, service ceiling of 18,400 ft., and max range of 540 miles. It is also equipped with in-flight refueling probe. HH-53s were used in the Son Tay Prison raid, and in the rescue of the Mayaguez crew. (All data for HH-53B. Follow on version, the HH-53C has larger T-64GE-7 engines which increase top speed to 196 mph and increase load to 18,500 lb.)

UH-1F of SOW at Hurlburt mounts rocket pod and minigun. Minigun is operated by gunner, while rockets are fired by pilot. (USAF)

UH-1F of 479th TFW, George AFB, Cal., 1975. (D. Kasulka via Norman E. Taylor)

UH-1N of 317th SOS, 1st SOW, Hurlburt Fld., 1971. The N model Huey is late version of the workhorse of Vietnam. It is powered by two P&W T400-PT-6 turboshaft engines. It can carry pilot and 14 passengers. Gross weight 10,500 lb. (R. Esposito via Norman E. Taylor)

UH-1N from the 24th Composite Wing, Howard AFB, Canal Zone, overflies Panama Canal during training flight. (USAF)

A-37 of 1st Special Operations Wing, 603rd SOS. (USAF)

(Above) "The Proud American", an A-1H of the 56th SOW, 602nd SOS early 1970. Though not fast, (top speed 311 mph at 18,500 feet) the A-1 was rugged and reliable and proved its worth throughout the Vietnam War, from beginning to end. (Neal Schneider via R.M. Hill)

(Below) A-1H of 4407th CCTS at Hurlburt in 1971. A-1 was powered by the Wright R-3350-26WA 18 cylinder engine, which developed up to 3,050 hp with water injection. Its cockpit was among the noisiest, hottest, and shakiest, but you felt secure behind all that thundering iron, and the airframe made for a rock-steady weapons delivery platform. (Jerry Geer)

(Above) A-1E of the 4407th CCTS, 1st SOW being armed for a mission on Eglin AFB range. TAC trained many Vietnamese pilots at Hurlburt, and the A-1 was their primary attack aircraft. (Author)

(Right) A-1E on the Hurlburt line in 1971. Handholds on fuselage sides were an absolute necessity for mounting the A-1, since the big R-3350 engine habitually coated the Skyraider's flanks with oil. (Jerry Geer)

(Below) T-28D of the 4407th CCTS at Hurlburt in 1970. The T-28 was pressed into COIN service when Counterinsurgency was the currency of the realm of anti-Communist activities. The T-28D-5 sported a strengthened wing which allowed it to carry a max ordnance load of 3,500 lb., including one fifty caliber machine gun in each wing. (F. MacSorley via Norman E. Taylor)

T-28 Specs

T-28D-5 was modified for close air support and Special Operations by the installation of the Wright R-1820-56S engine of 1,300 hp which gave it a top speed of 298 mph. at sea level. It also received two self-sealing fuel tanks of 174 gallons each, which gave it a range of 1,184 miles. It was first evaluated in combat in 1966 under USAF code name "Lucky Tiger".

T-28D-5 over Eglin AFB. TAC trained pilots of Laos, Thailand, Bolivia, and the Congo on the T-28. (USAF)

C-123K Provider of AFRES during operations conducted by 24th Composite Group, Howard AFB, Canal Zone. The 123, which became infamous because of its "Ranch Hand" herbicide defoliant spraying operations in Vietnam, was also used in operations such as this one, in which insecticide was used to reduce the Mediterranean Fruit Fly population in Nicaragua. (USAF)

DeHavilland U-6A of the 57th FWW, Nellis AFB, Nevada, 1971. (Swanberg via Geer)

Helio U-10A STOL aircraft used in numerous roles, including Psy-warfare leaflet drops, and delivery of supplies to Special Forces camps with minimal landing area. This U-10A belonged to 317th SOS, 1st SOW, Hurlburt Field, 1971. (Jerry Geer)

The Douglas A-26 became the B-26K in COIN operations. Supplied to the Vietnamese in the early sixties, it had the annoying habit of shedding its wings in high G pullouts. This was remedied by the remanufacturing process initiated by On-Mark Engineering Company. B-26s then returned to SE Asia and proved to be a devastating nemesis to traffic on the Ho Chi Minh trail in operations dubbed "Nimrod". Most eventually ended their careers in the Arizona desert, at Davis Monthan AFB storage facility. (Jerry Geer & Douglas Slowiak)

0-1 & 0-2 Specs:

Engine, Continental 0-470-11A of 213 HP. **Dimensions:** Span 36' Length: 25' 10" Gross Weight: 2,430 lb. **Performance:** Max Speed 115 mph. Range 530 miles. Developed for U.S. Army light liason and recconnaisance, 0-1 entered production in 1950. A total of 3,431 built. Military version of the popular Cessna 337 Skymaster series, the 0-2 was selected as the replacement for the 0-1 by the USAF in 1966. A total of 346 were ordered. The 0-2B, which was configured for Psy war operations, is no longer in use. Engines, two Continental 10-360-C/C of 210 HP eac. **Dimensions:** Span 38' 2", length 29' 9", height 9' 2". weights: empty 2,848 lb. gross 5,400 lb. **Performance:** max speed at sea level 199 mph, service ceiling 19,300 ft. range 1,060 miles. **Armament:** Four underwing pylons can carry light ordnance, including a 7.62 mm Minigun pod.

(Below) "Ronnie's Racer", an 0-1F of the 21st TASS at Tan Son Nhut AB Vietnam, 1970. (Norman E. Taylor)

The FAC

The Foward Air Controller has been around for a long time. In fact, since the American Civil War at least, when balloons were used for reconnaissance and artillery spotting. The role of FAC has never been more sharply defined or his tactics more refined than they are today. The dense jungle of Vietnam, combined with the absence, in most cases, of easily definable front lines, demanded the best possible control of high speed jet close air support aircraft. In Vietnam the FAC was one of the most hated, but respected, sights the enemy would see. On the one hand, they would have loved to have blasted him out of the sky. But, they knew what he could bring down on them if they revealed their positions to him. And that was often the FAC's only protection, for the nature of his job demanded a low and slow profile. With the exception of the high speed FACs who operated in North Vietnam, (which flew F-100Fs and F-4s because they knew they were going to get shot at regardless of what they flew.) they flew 0-1s, 0-2, and OV-10s. FACs assigned to a given province of Vietnam got to know the daily comings and goings of the populace, and could often spot enemy activity simply through the change of routine in their areas. In one of the ironies of modern aerial warfare, USAF FACs were drawn from the ranks of pilots at random. You might have flown a mach two Phantom, or a quarter of a million ton B-52 on the tour preceding your assignment to fly a 100 knot, one ton Bird Dog. The job was no less demanding and, in many cases, was much more hazardous.

0-1F of unkown unit over Vietnam sporting rather strange markings. (Note inverted insignia) (USAF)

0-2A of the 547th SOTS, 1st SOW, Hurlburt Field, 1972. (Norman E. Taylor)

0-2A of the 19th TASS at Tan Son Nhut AB, Vietnam, 1970. (USAF)

"Big Herb" of 21st TASS, Phu Cat AB, Vietnam, 1970. "Herb" was the call sign of the 21st. (Norman E. Taylor)

SSGT Dougherty parks "The Jefferson Airplane", an 0-2A of the 21st TASS at Phu Cat AB, Vietnam. It is armed with rocket pods used in marking targets for tactical fighters. (Norman E. Taylor)

0-2B of the 9th SOS, Phan Rang AB, Vietnam, 1970. (Norman E. Taylor)

0-2A taxies out for a mission from Phu Cat in 1970. 0-2 was never assigned an official nickname, but was known simply as "the Deuce". (Norman E. Taylor)

OV-10A Specs:

Engines, two Garrett Aireasearch T-76-G-416/417 turboprops of 715 hp each. **Dimensions:** span 40', length 41'7", height 15' 2". **Weights:** empty 6,969 lb, max gross 14,466 lb. **Performance:** max speed at sea level clean 281 mph, service ceiling 28,800 feet, combat radius with full load 228 miles. **Armament:** four fixed forward firing M-60C 7.62 mm machine guns mounted in fuselage sponsons. four hardpoints on sponsons capable of carrying up to 2,400 lb and one hardpoint under fuselage capable of carrying up to 1,200 lb. max weapons load 3,600 lb.

(Above & Right) OV-10A of the 4409th CCTS out of Hurlburt Field over the Gulf of Mexico during a 1972 FAC training mission. (Author)

OV-10A of the 4409th CCTS. Designed by North American for FAC mission and limited quick-response ground support, the OV-10 production run lasted only from 1967 to 1969. A total of 157 were acquired for USAF. (J. Finley via Norman E. Taylor)

TACTICAL ELECTRONIC WARFARE

Defined as a means to successfully penetrate hostile radar environments, complete the tactical mission, and return by employing electronic penetration aids, Tactical Electronic Warfare is one of the more mysterious missions of the Tactical Air Forces. Extensive use of EW dates back to the early days of World War II. Both Germany and Britain were developing radar, but neither had a very good idea of what the other had. In order to gather intelligence on British equipment, the Germans flew several Zeppelin missions in the North Sea area during 1939. The Zeppelins were equipped with sensitive radio intercept receivers. In one of those fortuitous flukes on which the fate of nations sometimes hangs, the receiver that was covering the British radar frequency was inoperative. The German operator, perhaps fearing reprisals, reported that his receiver showed that there were no signals. The Germans, already well on their way to being convinced that they were superior in all areas of modern warfare, simply assumed that the British were hopelessly behind in the development of high frequency radar. German research and development all but stopped. The immediate consequence of this action was the loss of the Battle of Britain. The long range consequences resulted in Allied penetration of the German radar network and devastation of the German homeland.

On a much smaller, but no less significant scale, similar consequences were suffered by our Tactical Air Forces during their initial penetrations of North Vietnamese air space in 1964-65. American EW efforts had been directed at strategic mission planning, which involved a one-time penetration and nuclear strike. When the tactical fighters started going downtown on a regular basis, it became painfully evident that they could not sustain the loss rates inflicted by a sophisticated and integrated radar-directed air defense system.

The immediate response to this threat was the reassignment of USAFE EB-66 jamming aircraft to PACAF. The EB-66s accompanied the strike force, providing radar jamming, and some threat warning. But the B-66 was itself too vulnerable to enemy fighters, and it was obvious that equipment would have to be developed that could be carried by the strike aircraft without degrading their weapons carrying capability.

The result of these needs has been a technological revolution in Tactical Electronic Warfare. Some of the more significant developments include RHAW (radar homing and warning) gear in the cockpit, self defense ECM pods that can be attached to the strike aircraft as needed, and an active method of combating the radar air defense network . . . the Wild Weasel.

Wild Weasel aircraft are equipped with more sophisticated radar detection gear, and carry missles that home on radar emissions, (Shrike or Standard ARM) as well as conventional ordnance to kill radar and gun crews. The Weasels became so effective in Vietnam that their very presence often was enough to cause enemy SAM sites to go "off the air" while the Weasels were in the area. Other EW ploys used in Southeast Asia included chaff and flares. (Chaff bombers would precede the strike force, laying a carpet of chaff to mask the presence of the strike force from enemy radar, while flares provided a simple but effective way to confuse heat-seeking missiles.)

The overall ECM effort during the Vietnam war was a dynamic and deadly game of cat and mouse. For, while we were working on ECM, they were working on ECCM! (Electronic Counter-Counter-Measures) Even though we clearly won the final big battle, (In which B-52s were able to range at will over the skies of what became known undisputedly as the toughest air defense environment in history through the coordinated use of ECM), it was evident that no nation could afford to rest on its EW laurels for long. If we needed further proof of this fact, the 1973 Mideast War demonstrated again what could happen to the best of the Air Forces if it let down its ECM guard.

TAC's Tactical Air Warfare Center, at Eglin AFB, Florida, is constantly working to improve the Electronic Warfare capabilities of Tac air. TAC is anticipating introduction of the F-4G advanced Wild Weasel aircraft, which will incorporate reprogrammable software to allow immediate countering of changing EW threats, advanced threat location gear which will assign priorities to the threats encountered, allowing for elimination of the most imminent danger first, and a new high-speed anti-radiation missle (HARM) which will permit stand-off attacks on air defense systems from outside the range of all known SAMs. Also enroute to TAC's EW inventory are TEREC (Tactical Electronic Reconnaissance, which locates and identifies threat radars) and PLSS (Precision Location Strike Systems) The EF-111A will have the speed, range, and self-defense capabilities to allow it to perform a wide variety of jamming missions. Electronic Warfare has become a fact of life in the 1970s Tactical Warfare scenario, and TAC will never again get caught with its electronic pants down.

(Above) EC-54D approaching Shaw AFB, S.C. in late 1969. (Jim Sullivan)

(Above & Below) EC-47P of the 361st TEWS taking off on a mission from Phu Cat AB, Vietnam in 1971. Many of the ECM aircraft, particularly those that operated in stand-off or relatively passive environments, were drawn from the mothball fleet. (Norman E. Taylor)

(Below) EB-66C of the 39th TEWTS, 363rd TRW, Shaw AFB, 1971. (Jerry Geer)

EB-66C of the 36th TFW, Spangdahlem AB, Germany, 1972. Douglas evolved the B-66 from the Navy's A-3 Skywarrior. It was originally intended to serve as a light bomber and reconnaissance aircraft. (D. Kasulka via Norman E. Taylor)

EB-66 Specs:

Engines, two Allison J79-A-13 turbojets of 10,200 lb thrust each. **Dimensions:** Span 72' 6", length 75' 1", height 23' 7". **Performance:** max speed 620 mph at 10,000 ft. Tactical radius with internal fuel 800 miles. Service ceiling 45,000 ft. Weights: empty 39,686 lb. max gross 79,000 lb.

EB-66E of the 39th TEWS taking off from Shaw AFB. A total of 209 B-66s were manufactured from 1954 to 1959. Scheduled to be phased out in the sixties, the B-66 was forced by events to soldier on into the seventies. (Norman E. Taylor)

EB-66E of the 39th TEWTS at Shaw in 1971. USAF originally intended to buy the A-3 "as is", but dictates of mission requirements forced extensive modifications that resulted in a completely new aircraft. (Jim Sullivan)

(Above Right) WB-66D of the 39th TEWTS at Shaw in 1970. During initial stages of "Rolling Thunder" operations against North Vietnam, the B-66 was used to provide ECM and Navigation for strike fighters. (Jim Sullivan)

EB-66E of the 39th TEWTS. (Jim Sullivan)

(Below Right) EB-66 en route to North Vietnam in the late sixties. (USAF)

EB-66E of the 42nd TEWS, 355th TFW at Takhli AB, Thailand in 1970. (Col. Don Kutyna)

EB-66 of the 42nd TEWS shows ECM antenna on fuselage sides as it gets away from Takhli for a mission over North Vietnam. (Col. Don Kutyna)

F-105G of the 66th FWS, 57th FWW, Nellis AFB, Nevada, 1973. (Norman E. Taylor)

F-105F Wild Weasel of the 44th TFS at Takhli in 1970. Weasels performed one of the most hazardous missions of the air war over North Vietnam, for it was their job to draw the SAM batteries into combat, then suppress them. (Col. Don Kutyna)

F-105F of the 419th TFTS, 23rd TFW "Flying Tigers" at McConnell AFB, Kansas, 1970. (Jerry Geer)

F-105G of the 35th TFW, 561st TFS, George AFB, California, 1975. (Jerry Geer)

F-105G of the 35th TFW. "G" model is the latest model of the two seat Wild Weasel Thud. It is operated by two regular Air Force squadrons. (Fred Roos via Norman E. Taylor)

(Below) ALQ-119 ECM pod carried by F-4 Wild Weasels is mounted beneath the forward Sparrow Missile well. (USAF)

F-105F/G Specs:

Span 34' 11", length 69' 7", height 20' 2". Weights: empty 27,500 lb. max loaded 54,027 lb. Other data similar to that of the F-105D. Principle difference between the F and G models is the QRC-380 ECM pods carried on fuselage sides.

Principle weapons carried by Wild Weasels were the AGM-45 Shrike and the AGM-78B Standard ARM. They are shown mounted on Thud at Takhli in Summer 1970. Both of these missiles home on radar emmissions. Performance of the Shrike is classified. Standard ARM has a top speed in excess of mach 2 and a range of 15 miles. F-105 Weasels also carried Cluster Bomb Units that were used on SAM site crews. If the enemy was quick enought to get his radar shut down before being zapped by one of the missiles, he still had to contend with the 105's Vulcan cannon and the CBUs. (Col Don Kutyna)

52nd TFW F-4Cs modified for the Wild Weasel role. They carry ALQ-119 pods and Shrike missiles. (USAF)

Wild Weasel F-4 also carries CBUs on centerline. Note modification to IR sensor under nose. (USAF)

F-4D of 52nd TFW taxies out for a mission in support of NATO from Spangdahlem AB, Germany. F-4s will take over the Wild Weasel mission completely from Thuds when the new F-4G Wild Weasel is operational. (USAF)

F-4G Wild Weasel version of the F-4 is a modified F-4E with sophisticated acquisition and jamming capability. (McDonnell Douglas)

The EF-111A, designed and built by Grumman Aerospace Corporation will provide any future strike force with superior jamming capability. (Grumman)

DC-130A of the 11th Tactical Drone Squadron, 355th TFW, at Davis Monthan AFB, AZ, 1973. It carries BQM-34A Firebee. (Norman E. Taylor)

DC-130 with full load of Firebees, configured for variety of missions.

BGM-34C under wing of DC-130. It carries 500 lb Snakeye Bomb and Maverick AGM. (USAF)

DC-130A of 11th TDS with AQM-34 underwing in 1971. (Norman E. Taylor)

R.P.V.s

Practically all of the present series of USAF RPVs trace their parentage to the twenty year old Ryan BQM-34A Firebee target drone. At least thirty distinct models have been derived from this remarkable airframe/engine combination. This variety of airborne drone hardware was spawned by the long and ever-changing air war in Southeast Asia. Operational RPVs in this series generally carry the designation AQM-34 or BGM-34 plus a letter suffix. Missions of RPVs include; Low altitude photo reconnaissance, the small size and fearlessness of the AQM-34M and AQM-34L make them highly effective in this role. Tactical electronic warfare support, RPVs can now be used as chaff bombers, preceding the strike force into the target area, laying a carpet of chaff to defeat enemy radars. They are capable of carrying mini-jammers for self protection, not only freeing strike aircraft to carry the ordnance, it is also transfering a highly hazardous mission to an expendable. Strike, the BGM-34C is capable of carrying smart and dumb bombs and can be used to hit high risk targets.

Though considered more expendable than manned aircraft in combat, the RPV's are always recoverable. Two methods exist at this time. In the first, the RPV is flown to the recovery area, the engine shut down, and a parachute is deployed to land it. This method usually results in some damage, and the alternative of using the MARS (Mid-Air Retrieval System) system is preferable. In this system, specifically configured helicopters are used to snare the RPVs recovery pilot chute and then reel in the RPV with a winch. This method is expensive and USAF is experimenting with air bags to cushion the landing of the RPV when descent is made with the recovery parachute.

RF-101C of the 29th TRS landing at Shaw AFB, SC (Jim Sullivan)

18th TRS RF-101Cs approaching Shaw for formation landing. (Jim Sullivan)

Prototype RF-101F, the ADC F-101B modified for Tactical Recce. (Jim Sullivan)

RF-101 Specs:

Engines, two P&W J-57-P-13 turbojets of 14,880 lb thrust with afterburning. **Dimensions:** Span 39' 8", length 69' 3", height 18' 0". Weights: max loaded 48,720 lb. **Performance:** max speed 1,120 mph at 40,000 feet, 716 mph at sea level. Initial rate of climb 14,000 fpm. Service ceiling 52,000 feet. max range (internal fuel) 1,700 miles at 595 mph at 36,000 feet. **Cameras:** one KA-1 framing, one vertical, two side oblique KA-2 framing, one CAI KA-18 strip.

RF-4 Specs:

Similar in performance to other USAF Phantoms, the RF-4 carries three basic reconnaissance systems, operated from rear seat, which include side-looking radar, an infra-red camera, and forward and side-looking cameras. A total of 505 RF-4s were built for USAF.

TACTICAL AIR RECONNAISSANCE

The reconnaissance mission is perhaps one of the least publicized, while extremely essential, missions of the Tactical Air Forces. TAC defines it as; "Mission of tactical air reconnaissance is to obtain accurate and timely information on enemy activities by visual, photographic, and electronic means." The information collected by tactical air reconnaissance is used by commanders of friendly units to destroy enemy forces, equipment and facilities. For this reason, the information must be passed on to the strike forces while it is still fresh.

The initial intelligence report for a tactical commander is obtained in flight when the reconnaissance aircrew relays its visual sightings via radio. (UHF or HF single sideband) The HF radio has an unlimited range capability and can be phone patched via AUTOVON to almost any location.

The "MISREP" is the written evaluation of the mission results and is ready for dispatch to the requesting military commander within 30 minutes after mission recovery.

The initial photo interpreter's report, or "IPIR", is ready for transmission within four hours after landing. This includes two contact prints of each target or sighting and the written intelligence evaluation of the target. Normally, original negatives of the mission would be ready within 45 minutes after mission recovery. Contact prints would be available two hours after landing.

During this decade, TAC has used a wide variety of reconnaissance aircraft, including the RF-101, RB-66, RF-4, and AQM-34L & M RPVs. The RF-101 is now in service with Air Guard units only. The standard reconnaissance aircraft in all of TAC's regular duty tactical recce squadrons is the RF-4.

To support the RF-4s and RF-101s, TAC reconnaissance wings employ the WS-430B Photo Processing and Interpretation Facility. (PPIP) It consists of 25 individual vans or shelters and is capable of processing, printing, duplicating and enlarging all the imagery produced by the varied sensors installed in the aircraft. Individual shelters of the WS-430B can be tailored or arranged for support of small six aircraft detachments or they can all be linked together to support elements up to and including an entire squadron. The individual shelters are portable and can be transported by tactical or strategic airlift aircraft.

RF-4C of 10th TRW, RAF Alconbury, England, 1976. (USAF)

Head-on of 10th TRW RF-4 shows forward looking camera window under nose. Inboard wing pylons are used for carrying ECM pods when missions are flown into high threat areas. (USAF)

(Above Right) RF-4C of 16th TRS, 363rd TRW, Shaw AFB, SC 1971. Recce pilots motto is "Alone, Unarmed, and Unafraid." (Jerry Geer)

(Below Right) RF-4C of the 67th TRW, Bergstrom AFB, TX adorned with Shark Mouth on nose, wing crest on intake. It carries Westinghouse ALQ-119 jamming pod under right wing. (Don Logan)

Illinois Air National Guard's 126th Air Refueling Wing flew KC-97Is and was assigned to TAC until 1977, when they traded in their 97s for KC-135s and became a SAC unit. (USAF)

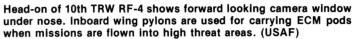

(Below) KC-97L of 126th ARW, Illinois ANG at Rhein-Main AB, Garmany, 1976. (Author)

ANG KC-97s support USAFE fighter units on a regular basis, making two to three week deployments to Rhein-Main AB, Germany. The Illinois Wing was the first to operate the KC-97L, and they did the initial flight testing of the jet engines on the KC-97. (Roger Besecker via Jim Sullivan)

The 98th Strategic Wing supports USAFE fighter units from Torrejon AB, Spain, with KC-135 Tankers. (USAF)

The 10th Airborne Command and Control Squadron is the only flying unit within the 513th Tactical Airlift Wing and is responsible for EC-135 Airborne Command Post aircraft and aircrews. (USAF)

EC-121H of the 79th Airborne Early Warning and Control Squadron at Homestead AFB, Florida, 1975. The 79th is the only Reserve unit flying the EC-121, which carries the Airborne Surveillance and Control System (ASACS) developed during the Vietnam war for the "College Eye" aircraft. ASACS gives EC-121 crews real time radar information. The EC-121 was flown on over 13,931 combat sorties, from 1965 to 1974, by the 552nd AEW&C Group, during which time they issued 3,297 MiG warnings, assisted in 25 MiG kills, and also assisted in 80 recovery assists of downed aircrew. In July 1976, the 552nd turned in their Connies and became the first unit to operate the Boeing E-3A AWACS. The E-3A is based on the 707-320B airframe, and carries a 30 foot rotating radar dome. It is capable of controlling any aspect of the air effort, including air superiority, strike, support, airlift, and interdiction. Its radar is able to detect and track low flying aircraft by eliminating ground clutter, a capability not now possessed in any other existing radar. The E-3A will portray broad and detailed battlefield status information through its impressive command-and-control communications capability. Data is gathered and portrayed by a deep-look, all-altitude surveillance radar and ancillary on-board computers, and will be downlinked to major command and control centers in rear areas or aboard ships via the Joint Tactical Information Distribution System, a secure, high-volume communications system. The critical elements of this information can then be forwarded to senior authorities in the U.S. in times of crisis. The E-3A carries a crew of 17, and has an endurance of more than 8 hours. (Bill Sides via Jim Sullivan and USAF)

HC-47A of the 12th TFW, Phu Cat AB, Vietnam, 1971. (Norman E. Taylor)

C-123K of the 311th TAS, 315th TAW, Phan Rang AB, Vietnam, 1971. (Norman E. Taylor)

C-47B of the 1st SOW, Hurlburt Field, 1974. Though not assigned to any regular airlift duties, the grande dame of aircraft continues to serve her masters in many ancillary duties. (Bill Sides via Jim Sullivan)

(Above, Above Left & Left) C-123K of the 310th TAS, 315th TAW, Phan Rang AB, 1971. The "Provider" was a derivitive of the Chase Aircraft designed glider, and served in many roles. "Patches", a DC-123K of the 310th was fitted with aerial spraying equipment. (Norman E. Taylor) The T-39A served as VIP transport for many TAC units. 92869 was assigned to the 66th FWS 57th FWW, Nellis AFB, 1972. (Jerry Geer)

(Below) C-7B Caribou of the 458th TAS, 483rd TAW, Cam Rahn Bay AB, Vietnam 1970. C-7 was used as a light Tactical Transport after being transferred from Army to Air Force. (Norman E. Taylor)

C-130E of the 24th Composite Wing. The Hercules is the backbone of Tactical Airlift Squadrons, whose mission remains the same after being transferred from TAC to MAC. (USAF)

C-130E of the 313th TAW making a rocket-assisted high-performance takeoff from Forbes AFB in 1972. (Fred Roos via Norman E. Taylor)

C-130E of the 348th TAS leaving Shaw AFB, SC in 1970. (Jim Sullivan)

Thunderbirds

The USAF Thunderbirds Aerial Demonstration Team is one of the most famous squadrons in the world. They have performed before millions of people in their illustrious twenty five year history. From 1969 through 1973 they flew the F-4E Phantom, one of the most impressive airshow airplanes ever. Despite the fact that the Phantom required a lot of room to maneuver, its size and the amount of noise it generated made it a real crowd pleaser. It proved to be a good Thunderbird airplane because of its power, and because its relatively large frontal area insured a quick deceleration when the throttles were retarded. But its size also meant that it was costly to operate and maintain, and when the energy crisis of 1974 hit, the Thunderbirds made a quick transition to the T-38A. The T-38 has proven to be one of the best airshow airplanes flown by any team. It is small and easily maintained. It has a roll rate that is nothing short of phenomenal, and good initial acceleration. And, since the Thunderbirds are in the business of selling young aspiring fighter pilots on the USAF, the Talon has another advantage. It is the trainer that all fighter pilots will fly before they graduate to a regular unit, so the young spectator's dream of flying the airplane the Thunderbirds use is well within reason.

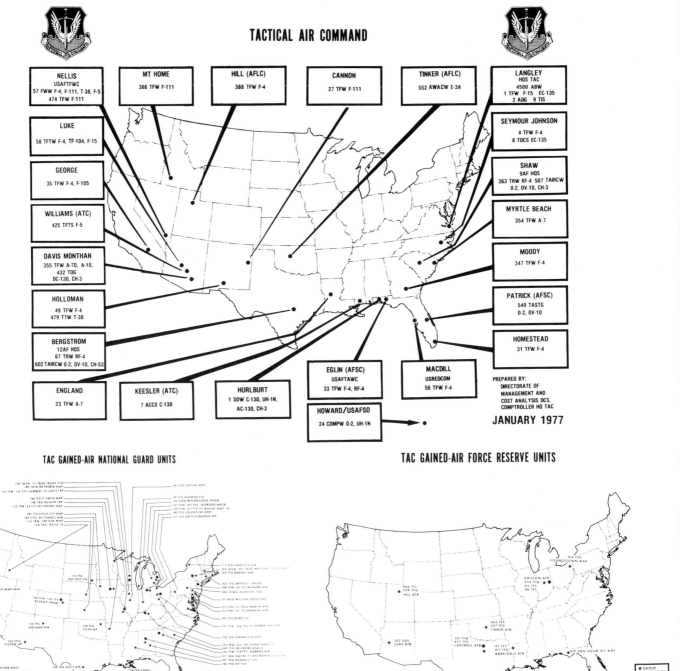

TACTICAL AIR COMMAND

NELLIS	USAFTFWC 57 FWW F-4, F-111, T-38, F-5 474 TFW F-111
MT HOME	366 TFW F-111
HILL (AFLC)	388 TFW F-4
CANNON	27 TFW F-111
TINKER (AFLC)	552 AWACW E-3A
LANGLEY	HQS TAC 4500 ABW 1 TFW F-15 EC-135 2 ADG 9 TIS
LUKE	58 TFTW F-4, TF-104, F-15
GEORGE	35 TFW F-4, F-105
WILLIAMS (ATC)	425 TFTS F-5
DAVIS MONTHAN	355 TFW A-7D, A-10, 432 TDG DC-130, CH-3
HOLLOMAN	49 TFW F-4 479 TTW T-38
BERGSTROM	12AF HQS 67 TRW RF-4 602 TAIRCW O-2, OV-10, CH-53
ENGLAND	23 TFW A-7
KEESLER (ATC)	7 ACCS C-130
HURLBURT	1 SOW C-130, UH-1N, AC-130, CH-3
EGLIN (AFSC)	USAFTAWC 33 TFW F-4, RF-4
MACDILL	USREDCOM 56 TFW F-4
HOWARD/USAFSO	24 COMPW O-2, UH-1N
SEYMOUR JOHNSON	4 TFW F-4 8 TDCS EC-135
SHAW	9AF HQS 363 TRW RF-4 507 TAIRCW O-2, OV-10, CH-3
MYRTLE BEACH	354 TFW A-7
MOODY	347 TFW F-4
PATRICK (AFSC)	549 TASTG O-2, OV-10
HOMESTEAD	31 TFW F-4

PREPARED BY:
DIRECTORATE OF
MANAGEMENT AND
COST ANALYSIS DCS,
COMPTROLLER HQ TAC

JANUARY 1977

TAC GAINED-AIR NATIONAL GUARD UNITS

TAC GAINED-AIR FORCE RESERVE UNITS

JANUARY 1977

JANUARY 1977